MW00668848

The Basilica of the Assumption

America's most historic place of worship

Baltimore, Maryland

Marty LaVor

*The James G. Robinson Foundation
has sponsored this book
in tribute to
Cardinal William H. Keeler
with sincerest thanks and appreciation for
his lifetime of service and leadership.*

opus fac evangelistae

In spite of the persecution they suffered during most of the eighteenth century, Catholics in America remained devout. After the American Revolution and the adoption of the constitution, which gave everyone the right to practice their religion openly, church leaders wanted to build a cathedral to reflect their devotion and new freedom to worship. John Carroll, the country's first bishop, later Archbishop of Baltimore, sought an architectural symbol that was "American" rather than the Gothic style traditionally found throughout Europe.

The United States Capitol at that time was the largest and most architecturally sophisticated building in America. The magnificent building was the work of Benjamin Henry Latrobe, the first professional architect and engineer to work in America. Benjamin Henry Latrobe, although not a Catholic, volunteered his architectural services for the new cathedral.

Latrobe presented Bishop Carroll with two plans: one Gothic, one Neoclassical. Carroll selected the Neoclassical design because of its similarity to the new U.S. Capitol in Washington and the design symbolically linked the two buildings. The skylights in the grand dome were key factors in Bishop Carroll's decision. The idea for the skylights that illuminate the Capitol came from Latrobe's friend, Thomas Jefferson. It was at Jefferson's insistence that Latrobe again used skylights in the dome of the new church. The result was an interior that was flooded with natural light from the skylights in the dome and the large windows located throughout the building.

Thus America's first Catholic cathedral, known as "the Basilica of the National Shrine of the Assumption of the Blessed Virgin Mary," was opened in 1821. With its grandeur, size and innovative design it clearly stood along side the U.S. Capitol as an equal.

Other than to say the Basilica has been significant in all aspects of the Catholic church in America for almost two centuries, the extensive history of the Basilica will not be written here. Instead, the focus is on the building itself and the results of the actions that were taken to save and restore it.

Unfortunately during the 180 years of the Basilica's existence many of Latrobe's grand designs and innovations were lost through "upgrades" and periodic maintenance. As a result of these alterations over the years many of the original prominent features either faded or vanished .

One of the most striking examples occurred during World War II, when, in 1942 the skylights of the dome were painted black for security purposes. By 1946, the window frames were so degraded that they, along with all of the heavy glass skylights of the outer dome, were removed. With no light coming in from above, combined with the forest green walls, black floors and brown pews that were installed during previous makeovers, the Basilica was quite dark.

In addition to very visible signs of deterioration, the infrastructure, including the electrical and heating systems of the building, had reached a critical point requiring replacement.

In 2004, Cardinal William H. Keeler, although not an architect, demonstrated insights that Benjamin Henry Latrobe would have admired when he decided to repair the Basilica and return it to the original design. Most people couldn't comprehend his vision. The critics could not understand why he wanted to remove the stained glass normally found in a church and replace it with clear glass. Few were aware that there had been glass in the original dome and his desire to put it back was part of the return to the original Latrobe concept. All these criticisms were dwarfed by his boldest idea - to put a chapel in the Basilica's undercroft. For 180 years, the great space, with its barrel vaults, inverted arches and spectacular masonry was used exclusively for storage.

Cardinal Keeler's vision was realized when in 2006, the breathtaking Basilica of the Assumption of the Blessed Virgin Mary, America's most historic place of worship, reopened.

This book is dedicated to Cardinal Keeler, with sincere thanks and God's blessings, not only for giving us this magnificent building once again, but also for his lifetime of leadership and service.

To begin to see the magnificence of the Basilica,

face the altar and then turn 360 degrees

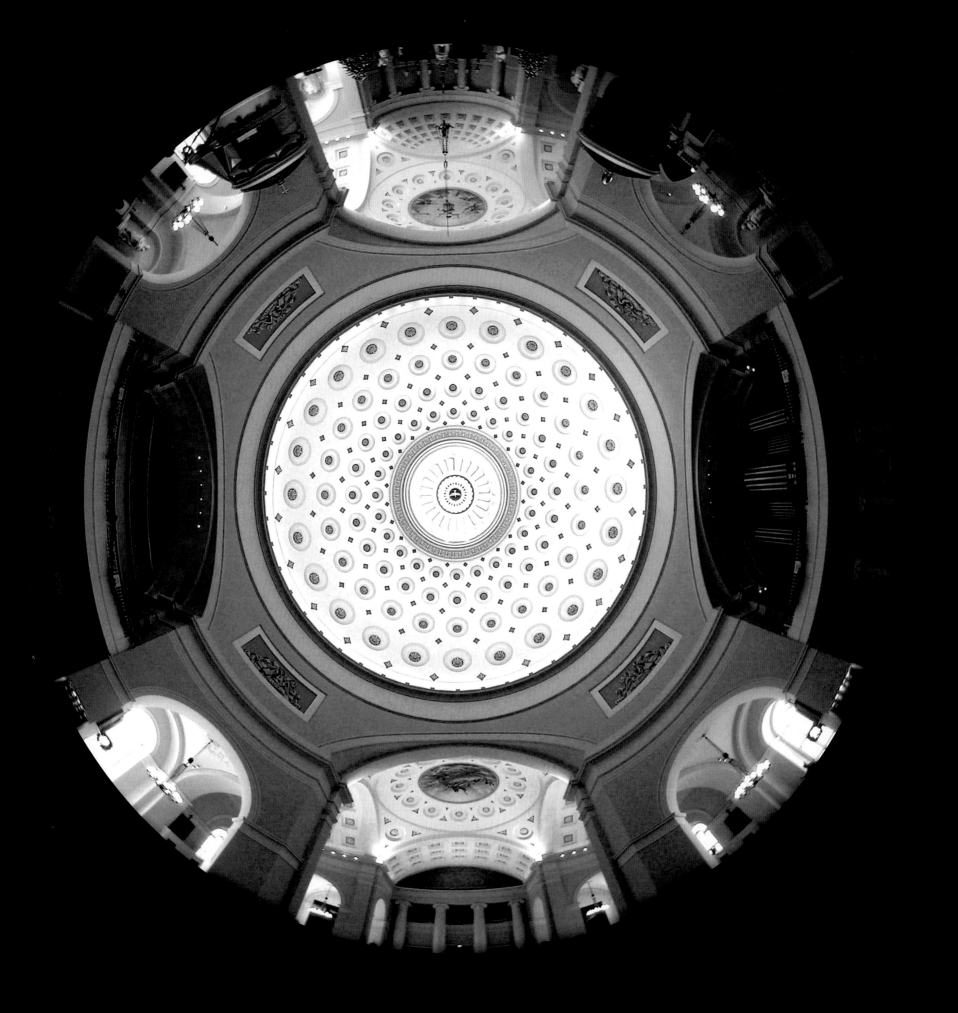

*Look up and see the
grandeur of the dome.*

*Begin with the
360 degree view.*

*Then imagine your eye is
a telescope as you look
at the next three images.*

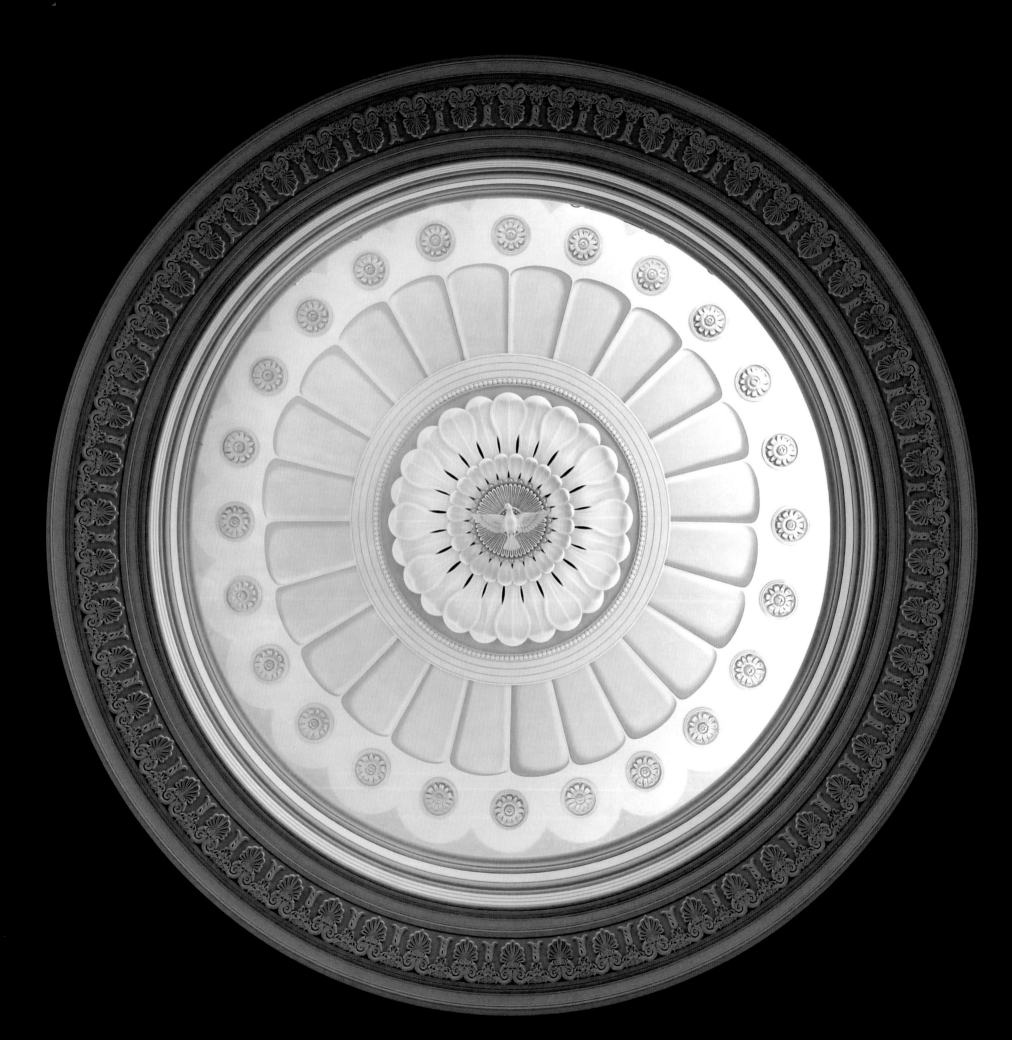

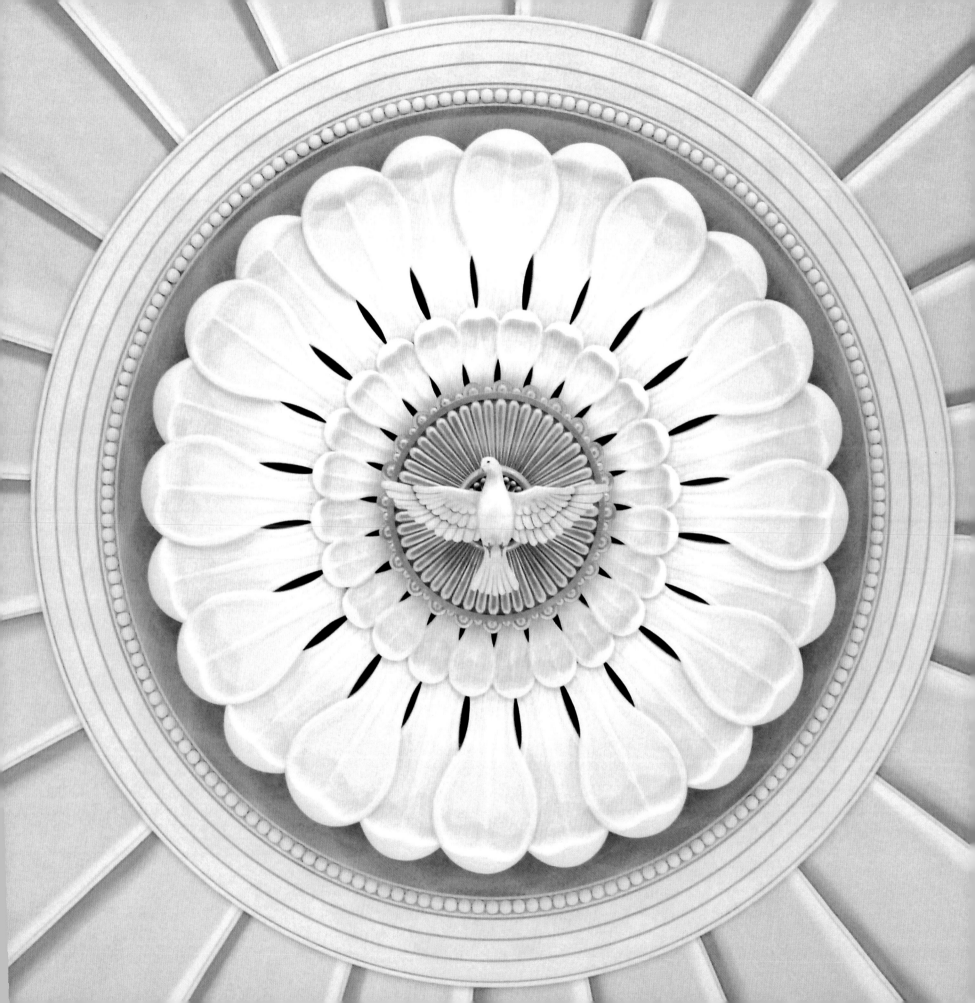

Outside the circle of the dome are the four panels of Saints Matthew, Luke, Mark and John

that were covered in 1865 and discovered intact during the renovation of the Basilica

Walk toward the entrance of the Basilica and look up.
You will see the breathtaking painting of the
"Assumption of the Blessed Virgin Mary"
on the West Saucer Dome.

The Dome is closed to the public.

Before the renovation, all twenty four skylights were covered,
the room was black and no light came into the Basilica from above.

Walk around the Basilica and see the sculptures, paintings, artifacts and memorabilia

IN MEMORY OF THE ARCHBISHOPS OF BALTIMORE
JOHN CARROLL
FIRST BISHOP AND ARCHBISHOP OF BALTIMORE
1790 — 1815
1815 LEONARD NEALE 1817
1817 AMBROSE MARÉCHAL 1828
1828 JAMES WHITFIELD 1834
1834 SAMUEL ECCLESTON 1851
1851 FRANCIS PATRICK KENRICK 1863
1864 MARTIN JOHN SPALDING 1872
1872 JAMES ROOSEVELT BAYLEY 1877
1877 JAMES CARDINAL GIBBONS 1921
1921 MICHAEL JOSEPH CURLEY 1947
1947 FRANCIS PATRICK KEOUGH 1961
1961 LAWRENCE CARDINAL SHEHAN 1974
1974 WILLIAM DONALD BORDERS 1989

JAMES CARDINAL GIBBONS
BORN JULY 23, 1834
ORDAINED PRIEST
JUNE 30, 1861
CONSECRATED BISHOP
AUGUST 16, 1868
NINTH ARCHBISHOP OF BALTIMORE
OCTOBER 3, 1877
CARDINAL OF HOLY ROMAN CHURCH
TITLE OF S. MARIA IN TRASTEVERE
JUNE 7, 1886
DIED MARCH 24, 1921.
A MILD AND PATERNAL RULER
OF HIS CLERGY AND PEOPLE
HONOR AND GLORY OF THE AMERICAN EPISCOPATE
MODEL OF EVERY CIVIC VIRTUE,
ADVOCATE OF THE WORKINGMAN
FRIEND OF THE POOR AND THE AFFLICTED
HE GOVERNED THE SEE OF BALTIMORE
FOR FORTY FOUR YEARS
IN JUSTICE, PEACE AND MERCY.

ERECTED BY HIS PRIESTS.
1924

The Basilica has been blessed by the visits of
Pope John Paul II and Mother Teresa.

HIS HOLINESS
PIUS XII
EUGENIO CARDINAL PACELLI

HERE KNELT IN PRAYER
OCTOBER 21, 1936

ELECTED POPE
MARCH 2, 1939

CROWNED POPE
MARCH 12, 1939

1634 · SOCIETY OF JESUS · 1805

IHS

1540

ANTISTITVM · SACRORVM

IN · STATIBVS · FOEDERATIS · AMER · SEPTENT

QVI · SVARVM · DIOECESIVM · RELIGIONEM

SPLENDIDIORI · FORMAE · REVOCATVRI

IN · CONCILIVM · PLEN · BALT · TERTIVM · CONGREGATI

PRAESIDE · IACOBO · GIBBONS · ARCHIEP · BALT

EX · LEONIS · XIII · P · M · DELEGATIONE

A · VI · ID · NOV · AD · V · ID · DEC · A · S · MDCCCLXXXIV

HOC · IN · TEMPLO · CONVENERVNT

IN · MEMORIAM · NOMINA · HEIC · RECENSENTVR

JACOBUS · GIBBONS · ARCHIEP · BALTIMOREN ·	PATRITIVS · A · FEEHAN · ARCHIEP · CHICAGINEN ·
PETRUS · R · KENRICK · S · LUDOVICI ·	GVLIELMVS · H · ELDER · CINCINNATEN ·
JOSEPHUS · S · ALEMANY · S · FRANCISCI ·	FRANCISCUS · X · LERAY · NEO · AVRELIANEN ·
JOANNES · B · LAMY · S · FIDEI ·	PATRITIVS · J · RYAN · PHILADELPHIEN ·
JOANNES · J · WILLIAMS · BOSTONIEN ·	MICHAEL · A · CORRIGAN · COADJ · NEO EBORACEN ·
CAROLUS · J · SEGHERS · OREGONOPOLITAN ·	PATRITIVS · G · RIORDAN · COADJ · S · FRANCISCI ·
MICHAEL · HEISS · MILWAUKIEN ·	JOANNES · SALPOINTE · COADJ · S · FIDEI ·
JOANNES · LOUGHLIN · EPISC · BROOKLYNEN ·	FRANCISCUS · S · CHATARD · EPISC · VINCENNOPOLITAN ·
LUDOVICUS · DE · GOESBRIAND · BURLINGTONEN ·	JOANNES · J · KEANE · RICHMOND ·
JOANNES · J · HENNESSY · DUBUQUEN ·	LAVRENTIVS · S · M·MAHON · HARTFORDIEN ·
EDUARDUS · FITZGERALD · PETRICULAN ·	JOANNES · VERTIN · MARQUETTEN ·
GULIELMUS · G · M·CLOSKY · LUDOVICOPOLITAN ·	EGIDIUS · JUNGER · NESQUALIEN ·
GULIELMUS · O'HARA · SCRANTONEN ·	MARTINUS · MARTY · O·S·B · VIC · AP · DAKOTE ·
BERNARDUS · J · M·QUAID · ROFFEN ·	JOANNES · B · BRONDEL · EPISC · HELENEN ·
TOBIAS · MULLEN · ERIEN ·	JOANNES · A · WATTERSON · COLVMBEN ·
JOSEPHUS · P · MACHEBEUF · VIC · AP · COLORADEN ·	PATRITIVS · MANOGUE · VALLIS·PRATEN ·
THOMAS · A · BECKER · EPISC · WILMINGTONEN ·	FRANCISCUS · JANSSENS · NATCHETEN ·
JOANNES · J · HOGAN · KANSANOPOLITAN ·	JOANNES · C · NERAZ · S · ANTONII ·
STEPHANVS · V · RYAN · C·M · BUFFALEN ·	KILIANVS · C · FLASCH · CROSSEN ·
JEREMIVS · F · SHANAHAN · HARRISBVRGEN ·	IGNANTIVS · M · WIGGER · NOVARCEN ·
CASPARUS · H · BORGESS · DETROITEN ·	MICHAEL · J · O'FARRELL · TRENTONEN ·
PATRITIUS · T · O'REILLY · CAMPI · FONTIS ·	HENRICUS · P · NORTHROP · CAROLOPOLITAN ·
LUDOVICUS · M · FINK · O·S·B · LEAVENWORTHEN ·	NICOLAUS · A · GALLAGHER · ADM · GALVESTON ·
FRANCISCUS · M·NEIRNY · ALBANEN ·	HENRICUS · T · RICHTER · FLUMINIS · RAPIDI ·
JOSEPHUS · DWENGER · C·PP·S · WAYNE · CASTREN ·	JOSEPHUS · RADEMACHER · NASHVILLEN ·
RICARDUS · GILMOUR · CLEVELANDEN ·	DIONYSIUS · BRADLEY · MANCESTRIEN ·
EDGARDUS · P · WADHAMS · OGDENSBVRGEN ·	HENRICUS · COSGROVE · DAVENPORTEN ·
THOMAS · F · HENDRICKEN · PROVIDENTIAE ·	CAMILLUS · P · MAES · EPISC · ELECT · COVINGTON ·
GULIELMUS · H · GROSS · C·SS·R · SAVANNEN ·	ALPHONSVS · J · GLORIEUX · VIC · AP · ELECT · IDAHEN ·
FRANCISCUS · MORA · MONTEREY · ET · ANGELOR ·	THOMAS · J · GRACE · EPISC · MENNEN ·
DOMINICUS · MANUCY · EPISC · ADM · MOBILIEN ·	EUGENIVS · O · CONNELL · JOPPA ·
JOANNES · J · KAIN · VELINGEN ·	JOANNES · J · CONROY · CURIOCEN ·
RUPERTUS · SEIDENBUSCH · O·S·B · VIC · AP · MINN · SEPTEN ·	
JACOBUS · A · HEALY · EPISC · PORTLANDEN ·	RICARDUS · PHELAN · V·G · PROCVRAT · EPISC · PITTSBVRG ·
FRANCISCUS · X · KRAUTBAUER · SINUS · VIRIDIS ·	FRANCISCUS · H · ZABEL · S·T·D · ALTONEN ·
JOANNES · IRELAND · S · PAULI ·	JOANNES · N · LEMMENS · ADM · VANCOVERIEN ·
JACOBUS · O'CONNOR · VIC · AP · NEBRASKA ·	BONIFACIUS · WIMMER · O·S·B · ARCHIABBAS · S·VINCENTII ·
JOANNES · L · SPALDING · EPISC · PEORIEN ·	EDUARDUS · SORIN · SUP · GEN · CONGR · S · CRVCIS ·
JOANNES · MOORE · S · AUGUSTINI ·	

BISHOPS CONSECRATED AT THE BASILICA OF THE ASSUMPTION
THE FIRST METROPOLITAN CATHEDRAL IN THE UNITED STATES

NAME OF BISHOP CONSECRATED	CONSECRATION DATE	FIRST EPISCOPAL ASSIGNMENT	PRINCIPAL CONSECRATOR
Benedict J. Fenwick, S.J.	November 1, 1825	Bishop of Boston	Ambrose Marechal, S.S.
John Dubois	October 29, 1826	Bishop of New York	Ambrose Marechal, S.S.
James Whitfield	May 25, 1828	Archbishop of Baltimore	Benedict J. Flaget, S.S. (Bardstown)
John Baptist Purcell	October 13, 1833	Bishop of Cincinnati	James Whitfield
Samuel Eccleston, S.S.	September 14, 1834	Coadjutor of Baltimore	James Whitfield
John J.M.B. Chanche	March 14, 1841	First Bishop of Natchez	Samuel Eccleston, S.S.
Richard V. Whelan	March 21, 1841	Bishop of Richmond	Samuel Eccleston, S.S.
William B. Tyler	March 17, 1844	First Bishop of Hartford	Benedict J. Fenwick, S.J.
William H. Elder	May 3, 1857	Bishop of Natchez	Francis P. Kenrick
John Barry	August 2, 1857	Bishop of Savannah	Francis P. Kenrick
J.M.P. Augustine Verot	April 25, 1858	Vicar Apostolic of Florida	Francis P. Kenrick
James Gibbons	August 16, 1868	Vicar Apostolic of North Carolina	Martin J. Spalding
Thomas A. Becker	August 16, 1868	First Bishop of Wilmington	Martin J. Spalding
Thomas P.R. Foley	February 27, 1870	Coadjutor and Apostolic Administrator of Chicago	William G. McCloskey (Louisville)
William H. Gross, C.SS.R.	April 27, 1873	Bishop of Savannah	James R. Bayley
Henry P. Northrop	January 8, 1882	Vicar Apostolic of North Carolina	James Gibbons
Alphonse J. Glorieux	April 19, 1885	Vicar Apostolic of Idaho	James Gibbons
Alfred A.P. Curtis	November 14, 1886	Bishop of Wilmington	James Cardinal Gibbons
Leo M. Haid, O.S.B.	July 1, 1888	Vicar Apostolic of North Carolina	James Cardinal Gibbons
John S. Foley	November 4, 1888	Bishop of Detroit	James Cardinal Gibbons
Placide L. Chapelle	November 1, 1891	Coadjutor of Sante Fe	James Cardinal Gibbons
Patrick J. Donahue	April 8, 1894	Bishop of Wheeling	James Cardinal Gibbons
Edward P. Allen	May 16, 1897	Bishop of Mobile	James Cardinal Gibbons
Henry Granjon	June 17, 1900	Bishop of Tucson	James Cardinal Gibbons
Thomas J. Conaty	November 24, 1901	Rector, Catholic University of America	James Cardinal Gibbons
Denis J. O'Connell	May 3, 1908	Rector, Catholic University of America	James Cardinal Gibbons
Owen P.B. Corrigan	January 10, 1909	Auxiliary Bishop of Baltimore	James Cardinal Gibbons
Thomas J. Shahan	November 15, 1914	Rector, Catholic University of America	James Cardinal Gibbons
William T. Russell	March 15, 1917	Bishop of Charleston	James Cardinal Gibbons
William J. Hafey	June 24, 1925	First Bishop of Raleigh	Michael J. Curley
Thomas J. Toolen	May 4, 1927	Bishop of Mobile	Michael J. Curley
John M. McNamara	March 29, 1928	Auxiliary Bishop of Baltimore and Washington	Michael J. Curley
Peter L. Ireton	October 23, 1935	Coadjutor and Apostolic Administrator of Richmond	Michael J. Curley
Jerome D. Sebastian	February 24, 1954	Auxiliary Bishop of Baltimore	Ameleto G. Cicognani, Apostolic Delegate
Michael W. Hyle	September 24, 1958	Coadjutor of Wilmington	Ameleto G. Cicognani, Apostolic Delegate

BISHOPS CONSECRATED AT ST. PETER'S PRO-CATHEDRAL

Leonard Neale	December 7, 1800	Coadjutor of Baltimore	John Carroll
Michael F. Egan	October 28, 1810	First Bishop of Philadelphia	John Carroll
Jean de Cheverus	November 1, 1810	First Bishop of Boston	John Carroll
Ambrose Marechal, S.S.	December 14, 1817	Archbishop of Baltimore	Jean de Cheverus

BISHOP CONSECRATED AT ST. PATRICK'S CHURCH
FELLS POINT, BALTIMORE

Benedict J. Flaget, S.S.	November 4, 1810	First Bishop of Bardstown	John Carroll

BISHOP CONSECRATED AT ST. ALPHONSUS CHURCH
BALTIMORE

John Nepomucene Neumann, C.SS.R.	March 28, 1852	Bishop of Philadelphia	Francis P. Kenrick
	June 19, 1977 Canonized Saint		

COUNCILS AND GATHERINGS OF BISHOPS IN THIS FIRST CATHEDRAL OF BALTIMORE

ESTABLISHMENT OF THE DIOCESE OF BALTIMORE, NOVEMBER 6, 1789
Pope Pius VI Established Baltimore as the First Diocese in the United States and Appointed John Carroll the First Bishop with the Mandate to Build this Cathedral

FIRST PROVINCIAL COUNCIL, OCTOBER 3 - 18, 1829
Archbishop James Whitfield Presiding, 5 Bishops in Attendance
Issued Decrees on Church Administration
Encouraged use of the Douay Version of the Bible
Asserted the Necessity of Catholic Schools

SECOND PROVINCIAL COUNCIL, OCTOBER 20 - 27, 1833
Archbishop James Whitfield Presiding, 9 Bishops in Attendance
Proposed the Formation of New Dioceses and Evangelization of Native Americans

THIRD PROVINCIAL COUNCIL, APRIL 16 - 23, 1837
Archbishop Samuel Eccleston Presiding, 9 Bishops in Attendance
Pastoral Letter Outlined Discrimination Against Catholics in the United States and
Assured American Civil Authorities of the Loyalty of Catholics

FOURTH PROVINCIAL COUNCIL, MAY 17 - 24, 1840
Archbishop Samuel Eccleston Presiding, 12 Bishops in Attendance
Enacted Laws for Mixed Marriages, Defined Jurisdiction of Pastors,
Counseled Temperance in Drinking and Promoted Catholic Education of Youth

FIFTH PROVINCIAL COUNCIL, MAY 14 - 21, 1843
Archbishop Samuel Eccleston Presiding, 15 Bishops in Attendance
Dealt with Sacramental Practice and Administrative Law Concerns

SIXTH PROVINCIAL COUNCIL, MAY 10 - 17, 1846
Archbishop Samuel Eccleston Presiding, 22 Bishops in Attendance
Declared the Blessed Virgin Mary Patroness of the United States
Under the Title of the Immaculate Conception

SEVENTH PROVINCIAL COUNCIL, MAY 6 - 13, 1849
Archbishop Samuel Eccleston Presiding, 1 other Archbishop, 23 Bishops in Attendance
Petitioned Pope Pius IX to Define the Immaculate Conception of the Blessed Virgin Mary

FIRST PLENARY COUNCIL, MAY 9 - 20, 1852
Apostolic Delegate: Archbishop Francis P. Kenrick
5 other Archbishops, 27 Bishops in Attendance
Extended the Legislation of the Seven Provincial Councils to the Entire Country

SECOND PLENARY COUNCIL, OCTOBER 7 - 20, 1866
Apostolic Delegate: Archbishop Martin J. Spalding
6 Other Archbishops, 37 Bishops in Attendance
Called for Evangelization of African Americans and for
a Greater Unity of Thought and Action Following the Civil War
President Andrew Johnson Attended the Final Solemn Session of the Council

THIRD PLENARY COUNCIL, NOVEMBER 9 - DECEMBER 7, 1884
Apostolic Delegate: Archbishop James Gibbons
13 Other Archbishops, 55 Bishops in Attendance
Commissioned the Baltimore Catechism
Began the Catholic University of America
Established Funding for African American and Native American Missions

CELEBRATION OF THE 100TH ANNIVERSARY OF THE ESTABLISHMENT OF THE DIOCESE OF BALTIMORE, NOVEMBER 10, 1889
James Cardinal Gibbons Presiding
1 Other Cardinal, 8 Other Archbishops, and 75 Bishops in Attendance
Archbishops Patrick J. Ryan of Philadelphia and John Ireland of St. Paul, Preachers

CELEBRATION OF THE 200TH ANNIVERSARY OF THE ESTABLISHMENT OF THE DIOCESE OF BALTIMORE, NOVEMBER 5, 1989
Agostino Cardinal Casaroli, delegate of John Paul II, Principal Celebrant
6 Other Cardinals, 33 Archbishops, and 270 Bishops in Attendance
Archbishop William Donald Borders, Chair, Bicentennial Committee, N.C.C.B.
Archbishop William H. Keeler, Homilist

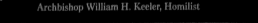

*The case organ, originally built in 1819,
was the largest and most elaborate in existance.*

During the renovation two balconies were discovered.

This is the view from the lower balcony that was used by freed slaves.

This is the view from the upper balcony that was open to the general public.

The view from the Pulpit

*The Cathedral
and the
Archbishop's
view from it*

opus·fac·Evangelistae

The Stations of the Cross

1. Jesus is Condemned to Die

2. Jesus Carries His Cross

3. Jesus Falls The First Time

4. Jesus Meets His Mother

5. Simon Helps Jesus Carry His Cross

9. Jesus Falls the Third Time

10. Jesus is Stripped of His Cloths

11. Jesus is Nailed to the Cross

6. Veronia Wipes Jesus' Face

7. Jesus Falls The Second Time

8. Jesus Speaks to the Women of Jerusalem

12. Jesus Dies on the Cross

13. Jesus is Taken Down From the Cross

14. Jesus is Laid in the Tomb

The high altar is known as the "Marechal Altar"

Above the Altar is a painting
of
"The Ascension of Jesus
into Heaven"

THE MASS VESTMENTS
WORN BY
ARCHBISHOP GIBBONS
AT THE 3RD PLENARY
COUNCIL OF BALTIMORE
NOV. 9 - DEC. 7, 1884

PIUS X

Pope Saint Pius X

CARDINAL
LAWRENCE J. SHEHAN'S
CAPPA MAGNA
"THE GREAT CAPE"

Visit the Basilica Museum and the Sexton House Gift Shop to see old vestments and original letters from Benjamin Henry Latrobe to Archbishop Carroll, plus others from U.S. Presidents.

Benjamin Latrobe offers his services
to Archbishop Carroll

Consecration of Bishop John Carroll notice

President Theodore Roosevelt to Cardinal Gibbons

JOHN,

By Divine Permission, and with the Approbation of the Holy See, Bishop of Baltimore,

To my beloved Brethren, the faithful of my Diocese, peace and the Blessing of our LORD JESUS CHRIST.

My beloved Brethren : Knowing, that you are mostly under the immediate charge and direction of virtuous and zealous Pastors, it did not appear to me necessary to add my frequent instructions to their useful lessons, and Christian exhortations : but, being required by the occasion, of which I shall now speak, to solicit your aid for the effecting of an important purpose, interesting the whole diocese, I cannot omit availing myself of it so far, as to renew the assurances of my solicitude for your progress in true Godliness and the exercises of a religious life, most conducive to your everlasting happiness. This is the first object, not only of the ministry committed to me by our Supreme Pastor and Lord Jesus Christ, but should be so of every act of my life, and particularly in my intercourse with you : It is the object of this address. Having long entertained an anxious desire of dedicating a Church to God, to be erected by the united efforts of all our Brethren in this Diocese, to stand as the evidence of their attachment to the unity of episcopal government, as well as of their unity in faith, (for these are inseparable ;) and being made duly sensible by my descent into the vale of years, that I ought not to expect to see this work accomplished, unless it be soon undertaken ; I am induced to recur to, and intreat you, by your attachment to the interests of our holy religion, and affection for its Author, and the object of its worship, Jesus Christ, to lend your aid towards carrying this design into effect.

The particular exigencies of every Congregation for building and preserving their churches and places of worship, and affording a subsistance to their Pastors, forbid the expectation, and even the desire of ample contributions from the generality of our Brethren, living at a distance from the Seat of the intended Cathedral : But who are there amongst you, that cannot, without inconvenience to yourselves, manifest your good dispositions for the advancement of God's glory, and your admiration of the examples left by our Catholic Brethren in all those countries, on which the rays of true reli-

Bishop Carroll's appeal for funds to build
the Basilica June 23, 1803

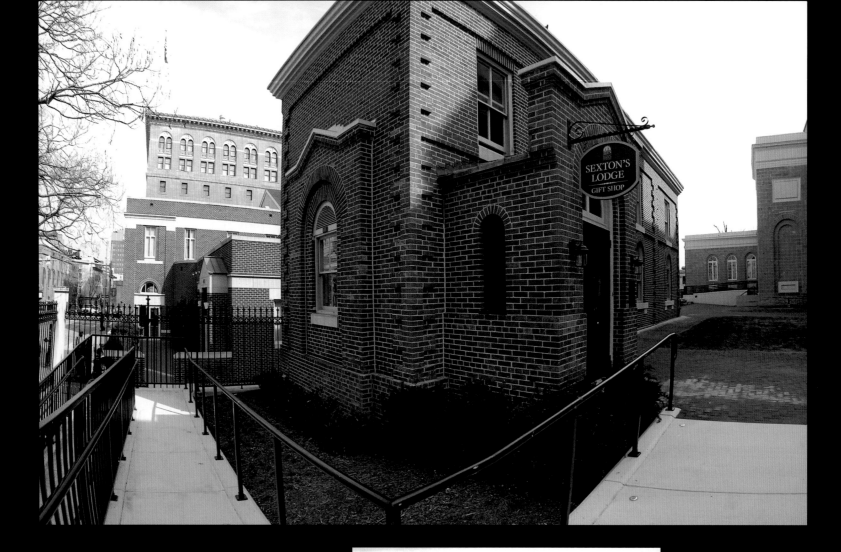

THE WHITE HOUSE
WASHINGTON

16 May, 1918

My dear Cardinal Gibbons:

I am very much interested in the request you make in your letter of yesterday and write now simply to assure you that I will look into the matter very carefully and will do anything that it is within my legal power to do. The matter had not been brought to my attention, and I will inform myself of the possibilities under the law at once.

Thanking you for your letter,

Cordially and sincerely yours,

Woodrow Wilson

His Eminence,
J. Cardinal Gibbons,
Baltimore, Maryland.

His Eminence
John, Cardinal Gibbons,
Baltimore, Md.

Your Eminence:

I am deeply obliged to you for your kind letter of September 25, 1920 and shall, as you suggest, get in touch at once with the Archbishop of New York. Please accept my warm thanks for your prompt offer of cooperation. I sincerely hope that co-ordinate action by the various relief associations in this country will help relieve the terrible distress of the suffering children in Central Europe.

Yours faithfully,

Herbert Hoover

HH.A

PROPOSALS
FOR A
SUBSCRIPTION,
TO BUILD A
CATHEDRAL CHUR[CH]

At BALTIMORE, and for purchasing sufficient Lots
for that and other necessary Purposes.

LITTLE need be said to evince the expediency and neceſſity of carrying into effect...

To the Roman Catholics in the
United States of America.

Gentlemen.

While I now receive with much
satisfaction your congratulations on my being
called, by an unanimous vote, to the first
station in my country; I cannot but duly
notice your politeness in offering an apology
for the unavoidable delay. As that delay
has given you an opportunity of realizing,
instead of anticipating, the benefits of the
general Government; you will do me the
justice to believe, that your testimony of the
increase of the public prosperity, enhances the
pleasure which I should otherwise have
experienced from your affectionate Address.

I feel that my conduct, in war
and

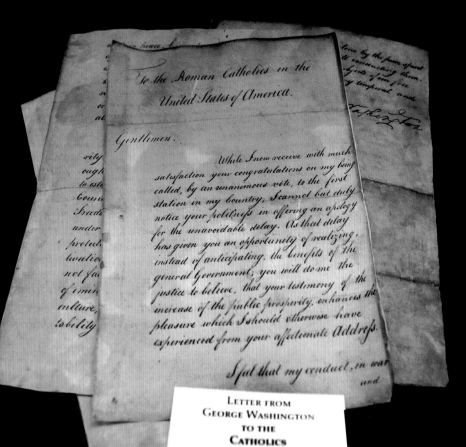

PIVS PP. VI

AD FVTVRAM

REI MEMORIAM

THE UNDERCROFT

When Benjamin Henry Latrobe planned the Basilica he envisioned a chapel in the Cathedral's great Undercroft, the level below the sanctuary. Unfortunately, his plan was abandoned when construction workers built the floor too high. To compensate for the mistake of the high floor, Latrobe had to add unusual inverted arches.

For 180 years, this great space with its barrel vaults, inverted arches and spectacular masonry was used exclusively for storage.

As part of the renovation of the Basilica, workers removed tons of sand, which was the base material used by Latrobe. For the first time the amazing brickwork was seen. Because the electric light did not exist when the original construction took place, the addition of dramatic lighting has made the Undercroft breathtaking beyond Latrobe's wildest dreams.

The most important feature of the Undercroft is the new Our Lady Seat of Wisdom Chapel.

ST. MARY'S SEMNARY IN THE 19TH CENTURY

In 1790 Bishop John Carroll invited Sulpicians to come from France to found the first Catholic Seminary in the United States ~ St. Mary's Seminary & University. After their arrival in 1791, the Sulpicians advised Bishop Carroll on the selection of the site for his cathedral and assisted him in raising funds for its construction.

In 1821 the Cathedral was dedicated by Archbishop Ambrose Maréchal, a Sulpician, who, along with another Sulpician, Archbishop Samuel Eccleston, is entombed adjacent to this chapel.

During the 19th century Sulpicians were ordained bishops in this church to provide leadership for new dioceses. The nearby St. Mary's Seminary was the site of many working sessions of the Church councils held at the Basilica. For many generations, until the Seminary relocated to Roland Park, seminarians and faculty members from St. Mary's assisted at liturgies here.

ARCHBISHOP MARÉCHAL

This crypt chapel, dedicated to Our Lady Seat of Wisdom, was a gift of the Sulpician Fathers to the Basilica of the Assumption in recognition of their long and significant relationship with this great church and the Archdiocese of Baltimore.

It is with great gratitude to the Church of Baltimore that the Sulpicians supported the effort led by His Eminence William Cardinal Keeler to restore the Basilica in accord with the vision of its original designer Benjamin Henry Latrobe.

This plaque was dedicated on November 10, 2006, by Lawrence B. Terrien, S.S. Superior General of the Society of St. Sulpice

Plaque 1

Hic jacet

Illus.mus et Rev.mus D.D. Pater in Xsto.

MARTINUS JOANNES SPALDING,

septimus Archiepiscopus Baltimorensis,

natus XXIII Maii MDCCCX,

electus ad Sedem Ludovicopolitanam,

X Septembris MDCCCXLVIII,

translatus ad Sedem Balt. VI Maii MDCCCLXIV,

aetatis suae anno IXII.

obiit VII Februarii MDCCCLXXII.

Maxima pietate et doctrina, necnon paupe etate
Archiepiscopalem cathedram exornuit.

R. I. P.

Plaque 2

Hic jacet

Illustrinus ac rev.mus D.D. Pater in Xsto.

FRANCISCUS PATRITIUS KENRICK

sextus Archiepiscopus Baltimorensis

natus die III Decembris A.D. MDCCXCVII

electus Episc. Arath. die XXV Feb. MDCCCXXX

translatus ad sed. Philad. die XXII Apr MDCCCXLII,

ad sed. autem Balt. die XIX Aug. MDCCCLI

vita functus die VIII Jul. A.D. MDCCCLXIII

aetat. suae an. LXVI.

Maxima pietate et doctrina, necnon pari modestia et paupertate
Archiepiscopalem cathedram exornavit.

R. I. P.

Plaque 3

Hic apponuntur mortales exuviae

AMBROSII MARECHAL,

Archiepiscopi Baltimorensis, nati die quintâ

Decembris 1768, Consecrati Archiepiscopi

Baltimorensis, die decima quarta Decembris

1817, qui obiit die vigesima nonâ Januarii 1828.

ORATE PRO EO.

Plaque 4

Intus jacet

JACOBUS WHITFIELD

qui natus in Angliâ die 3ª Novembris, A.D. 1770,

consecratus vero Archiepiscopus quartus Baltimorensis

die 25ª Maii, A.D. 1828,

obiit die 19ª Octobris, A.D. 1834.

R. I. P.

Hic ✝ jacet

REVᵐᵘˢ SAMUEL ECCLESTON,

quintus Archiepiscopus Baltimorensis:
natus in Statu Marylandiensi die 27 Junii A.D. 1801;
Sacerdos factus A. 1825; Præses Collegii S. Mariæ
Baltimoren. A. 1829; Episcopus consecratus cum titulo
Coadjutoris A. 1834; eodem anno Archiepiscopus renuntiatus; Doctrina, zelo, pietate ac morum suavitate con-
spicuus; Obiit die 22 Aprilis, A.D. 1851.

R. I. P.

Hoc Sepulcro
reconditur corpus
JOANNIS CARROLL
primi Archiepiscopi
BALT.
defuncti 3ᵈ Decembris
1815.

Hic jacet

JACOBI GIBBONS

S.R.E. Presbyteri Cardinalis

Tit. Sanctae Mariae in Trans Tiberim

Archiepiscopus Baltimorensis

Natus die 23 Julii 1834

Obiit die 24 Martii 1921

R. I. P.

Hic ✝ jacet

MICHAEL JOSEPH CURLEY

Archiepiscopus Baltimorensis et Washingtonensis
Natus die 12a Octobris 1879
Sacerdos factus die 19a Martii 1904
Episcopus Scti Augustini consecratus die 30a Junii 1914
Ad Sedem Archiepiscopalem Baltimorensem
provectus die 10a Augusti 1921
Sedis Washingtonensis noviter erectae
Archiepiscopus renuntiatus die 22a Julii 1939
Obiit die 16a Maii 1947.

The Archbishop's Residence

Offices and Meeting Rooms

Built eight years after the Basilica was completed, the Archbishop's residence, offices and receiving rooms, serve as a working extension of the Basilica. Although the Cardinal and the Basilica's pastor live there, the building is used daily for meetings, lunches, dinners and receptions with people from Maryland as well as dignitaries from around the world.

His Holiness, Pope John Paul II used it during his visit to Baltimore in 1995.

The building is decorated primarily with portraits of Cardinals and Archbishops who served the Archdiocese. Most of the artwork was given as gifts more than 100 years ago.

The Dining Room

The Gibbons Room

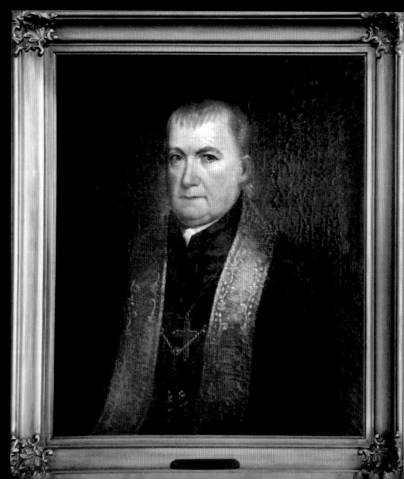

POPE JOHN PAUL II
PRESENTED TO THE ARCHDIOCESE OF BALTIMORE

*The Archbishop's
Office*

The Reception Rooms

With the Compliments of

KING HUSSEIN I

HOLY BIBLE

CONTAINING BOTH THE OLD AND NEW TESTAMENTS

RED LETTER EDITION

THE NEW AMERICAN BIBLE

Translated from the Original Languages
with Critical Use of All the Ancient Sources
by
members of the Catholic Biblical Association of America

SPONSORED BY THE BISHOPS' COMMITTEE
OF THE
CONFRATERNITY OF CHRISTIAN DOCTRINE

THOMAS NELSON PUBLISHERS
Nashville • Camden • New York

The Archbishop's Chapel

The upper and lower halls

In 1982, Marty LaVor turned a hobby into a career and became a full-time freelance photojournalist. Since then he has taken over 950,000 photographs. He travels extensively and has photographed in over 100 countries, specializing in candid work. His photographs are used in newspapers, magazines, newsletters, corporate reports, political campaigns, posters and books. He has had 35 one-man exhibitions and his work is held in private collections throughout the world.

Books by Marty LaVor

o   Marty taught himself to use a camera in 1960 when he wrote a "how to" book for hobby ceramics. It became the basic instruction guide for the industry. "CERAMICS FOR ANY HANDS" contained 400 close-up photographs, had six printings and was on the market for twenty-five years.

o   In 1990, he produced his first photography book "NO BORDERS." It won the "Best Book Award" from Studio Magazine International and "Best in Show-Grand Prize" from the Printing Industries of Maryland.

o   His second photography book, with over 350 photographs, documented "The VIII Plenary Session of the Theological Dialogue between the Catholic Church and the Orthodox Church," won a major award from the Printing Industries of America National Competition.

o   His third and fourth photography books "Washington See It Again For The First Time Looking Up" and "The Capitol See It Again For The First Time Looking Up" also received critical acclaim.

o   His fifth book "NO BULL!" was called the "best book ever done on the Cheyenne Frontier Days rodeo."

o   He also wrote two non-photography books and had over 100 articles published in professional journals.

Prior to his career as a professional photographer, Marty LaVor had already achieved an impressive list of personal accomplishments. He earned a Doctorate in Special Education, was an Industrial Arts teacher, a department head of a public school, Executive Director of a rehabilitation training program for retarded and physically handicapped women, Senior Professional for the Alabama Technical Assistance Corporation, Senior Federal Regional Officer for the Southeast Office of Economic Opportunity, Senior Professional Staff member for the U.S. House of Representatives Education and Labor Committee, Consultant to the U.S. Senate Committee on Aging, and Consultant to the U.S. House of Representatives Select Committee on Hunger. After he retired from the U.S. Congress he established The LaVor Group, specializing in political and public services.

"The Basilica of the Assumption"

The LaVor Group   7710 Lookout Court   Alexandria, Virginia 22306

Marty LaVor's website: www.martylavor.com